INDIAN HOMES

Troll Associates

INDIAN HOMES

by Keith Brandt

Illustrated by George Guzzi

Troll Associates

Library of Congress Cataloging in Publication Data

Brandt, Keith, (date)
Indian homes.

Summary: Describes the characteristics of the different
types of dwellings used by various Indian tribes through-
out North America.
1. Indians of North America—Dwellings—Juvenile lit-
erature. [1. Indians of North America—Dwellings]
I. Guzzi, George, ill. II. Title.
E98.D9B75   1984   392'.36'008997   84-2650
ISBN 0-8167-0126-1 (lib. bdg.)
ISBN 0-8167-0127-X (pbk.)

All of the Indian tribes in North America were descended from people who migrated from Asia at least fifteen thousand years ago. But time brought changes. And as the Indians spread out over the huge continent, they developed many different ways of living. Even the homes they built varied from tribe to tribe.

A number of factors determined the kind
of home a particular Indian tribe used. The
first was *climate*. Tribes that lived in cold,
snowy, or icy places built dwellings that
would keep out the freezing winds and
snow. Tribes that lived where the weather
was warm all year built the coolest possible
living quarters. Where the ground was wet
and swampy, Indians built homes that were
raised up off the ground on stilts.

What building materials were available also determined how Indians built their homes. For example, wood was scarce in the Southwest, so the tribes that lived there used mud and brush and sod. But since wood was plentiful in the Northwest, the tribes that lived there had houses made of planks.

Another factor was *the length of time the home was to be used.* Tribes that stayed in one place all the time built sturdy, permanent dwellings. Nomadic tribes that wandered from place to place built homes that could be put up, taken down, and carried very easily.

The nomadic Plains tribes that hunted buffalo and deer used animal hides as their building material. The Eastern Woodlands Indians, who farmed in one place until the land stopped producing crops, built homes that would last about as long as the crops kept coming. If they feared attacks from other tribes, they often surrounded their homes with a stockade of wooden posts.

Other factors that affected the kind of home included *tribal customs and way of life.* In some tribes each family had its own dwelling. In other tribes a number of families lived together. Some tribes had different winter and summer dwellings. Still others traditionally made their homes partly underground.

One thing that many, though not all, tribes had in common was that the entrances to their homes faced east. There may have been some religious reason for this, or it may have been done to let in the first light of day as the sun came up.

A belief shared by all Indians was that nobody owned the land. The land belonged to the Great Spirit, and its resources were there to be used by all people.

Before the settlers came, the North American population was small, and the land was vast and open to everybody. Very few tribes had permanent homes.

The first Indians encountered by the early settlers were tribes of the Eastern Woodlands. Among them were the Mahican, Algonquin, Chippewa, Iroquois, and Delaware.

The Iroquois were known to the settlers as the "Five Nations," because they were actually five separate tribes—but they called themselves the "People of the Long House."

The Iroquois lived in semi-permanent villages near their farm fields. After about ten years, when the soil no longer produced good crops of corn, squash, and beans, the tribe would move to a new place not far from the old one.

By the time the soil was worn out, two other things had happened. First, the supply of firewood in the area had been used up. And second, the bark that covered the Iroquois long houses had become bug-infested and had begun to decay. But with so much fertile, unused land available, it was an easy matter for a tribe to set up a new village nearby and start over.

The largest long houses were often about half as long as a football field. Inside the building was an open area with double bunks lining both sides. Each bunk was about the size of two king-sized beds. Parents slept on the bottom bunk, the children slept on the bunk above. Each family's possessions were kept on the bunks and on the floor.

Some long houses were smaller. The length of the long house depended on the size of the "extended family" that lived in it. An extended family included grandparents, parents, brothers, sisters, cousins, uncles, and aunts.

Each family within the extended family did its cooking over an open fire. The fire was set in the center space of the house, right in front of their bunks. The smoke from all the fires drifted up and most of it escaped through holes in the roof—but not all. And those families that had bunks in the middle of the long house always had to breathe thick smoke.

The Mahican, Algonquin, Chippewa, and other Woodlands tribes built homes called wigwams. They were made of poles covered by tree bark, but they were smaller than Iroquois long houses, and they were shaped differently. The Mahican, Algonquin, and Chippewa built dome-shaped wigwams, which looked like large bowls turned upside-down.

A single family lived in a wigwam. In the center was an open fire. Around it were wooden platforms, set like couches against the circular wall. These platforms, covered by woven grass mats and animal skins, were used for sitting and sleeping.

On hunting trips the Woodlands Indians set up cone-shaped wigwams for temporary use. These were made of poles and bark, and looked like the teepees of the Plains Indians.

Among the Plains Indians of the Midwest were the tribes of the Sioux Nation. Their teepees were made of twenty-foot-long cedar or pine poles, covered by buffalo hides sewn together.

The poles were lashed to each other at the top, forming a structure like an upside-down ice-cream cone. The skins did not reach the point of the cone. This left an open space at the top through which smoke from the cooking fire could escape.

Because the Plains Indians were nomadic hunters, their homes had to be light and collapsible. Their teepees could be put up and taken down quickly, and there was no permanent furniture to carry about. Plains Indians slept on grass pads covered with buffalo skins. These also could be rolled up and carried easily.

Some tribes of the Plains did live in permanent homes. The Mandans, for example, built solid, dome-shaped lodges. The Mandans were primarily farmers and did not travel far from their fields of grain and corn.

Their lodges were made of wooden posts and beams, covered with a layer of thatch, which is dried grass and reeds. On top of the thatch was a layer of turf. Turf is the top layer of the soil, held together by grass and roots. The Mandan earth lodge was a very strong, durable structure.

Inside a Mandan home was one large room, with an open fire burning in the center. The Mandans found a clever way to create privacy in their one-room homes. They built four-poster beds and covered them with curtains of buffalo hide. A curtained bed made a warm, comfortable nook for sleeping and relaxing.

In warmer climates, homes were designed to be as cool as possible. The Indians of the Southeast were mostly farmers who had well-ventilated homes.

Among them were the Seminoles, who lived in open huts. These were often little more than wooden platforms, raised off the ground. They had a thatch roof and either partial walls or no walls at all. The raised platform let air circulate through and under the hut. It also kept the floor from rotting in the hot, wet climate.

Indian tribes of the Southeast often built a completely closed house, called a winter lodge. It served as a kitchen all year round and as a sleeping place during cold weather.

The Indians of the hot, dry Southwest, such as the Hopi, were also farmers who lived in permanent homes. Their dwellings looked like modern apartment buildings, with many rooms and terraces.

These dwellings, called pueblos, were made of stone or adobe. Adobe is hard, dried mud. The pueblos were built against the side of a mountain, in an open area, or on a high mesa, which is a flat-topped hill.

To build their adobe homes, pueblo-dwellers erected a frame of wooden poles. Next, they stretched animal skins from pole to pole, inside and outside. Then mud was poured into the space between the skins and the poles. It was similar to the way modern builders pour concrete into hollow forms. When the adobe was dry and hard, the skins were removed.

A pueblo roof had a hole in it, to let out smoke from the cooking fire below. The same hole was used as a door to and from the room. To reach the roof from the outside, an Indian had to climb a wooden ladder. This ladder always leaned against the wall except when an enemy tribe attacked the town. Then the ladder was taken inside.

To climb into and out of a room, an Indian used a notched pole. It leaned against an inside wall and led directly to the roof hole. The roof itself was used a lot in the dry, hot climate of this region. It was a cool area for household work, relaxing, and sometimes for sleeping.

The second floor of a pueblo was not built right on top of the first floor. It was set back and entered by a ladder that stood on the first-floor roof. When a second story was added to a pueblo, the first-floor space below it got no light. Still, it made a cool storage area.

In the Northwest, near the Pacific Coast, the rich forests yielded an endless supply of wood. For that reason, the Kwakiutl and Haida tribes built lodges totally of wood.

Each lodge housed an entire extended family and was quite large. A Haida house might be one hundred feet long and forty feet wide. At the corners there were heavy log posts. These were supports for the roof beams.

At the center of the outer wall along one side of the house stood an even taller post. It was carved all over with designs, called totems, that told the history of the family. There was a hole carved right through the center post at ground level. This was the lodge door. The totem pole was believed to have magical qualities.

As settlers moved across the continent, pushing the Indians from their lands, many of the traditional homes of the Indians disappeared. Today, interest in the culture of the North American Indian has grown. And with this increased interest, students of Indian life are examining in great detail the fascinating homes in which the North American Indians once lived.